Creation Yoga

Author and Illustrator
Kendra Hunt

Creation Yoga

Author and Illustrator
Kendra Hunt

Creation Yoga is dedicated to
my friends, and my mom, Ginger. She wrote three books
and taught me when she was in pain.

Yoga is a love at first sight for me. Hopefully it will be helpful for you.

Downward-facing Dog Pose

I think of all the dogs I've had when I do this pose.
Galvin, Ella, and Bella.
They all wanted to escape! Ella was the one who did it most! Galvin was the calmest and least who escaped! Yeah, Ella!!

Mountain Pose

Yoga makes me feel like life is good so make it sweet like a Mountain.

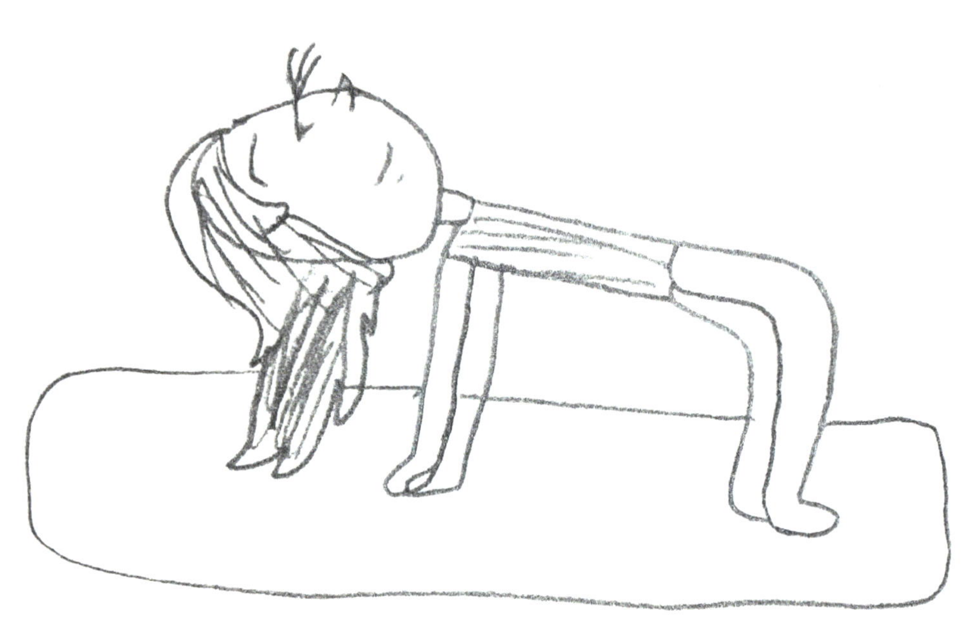

Crab Pose

Crab pose you can try to balance a stuffed animal on your stomach. It takes me to the place I was born, Florida! Beaches, white sand, ocean, then we have the... CRABS! They're harmless until you step on them. So, watch your step, children!

Rainbow Pose

Rainbow pose is just like bridge, what gymnasts do. It looks like a rainbow if you have your red, orange, yellow, green, blue, and purple colors!

Butterfly Pose

Butterfly pose is as if you're a beautiful butterfly fluttering in the wind. But you sit on the floor though. It makes me feel great.

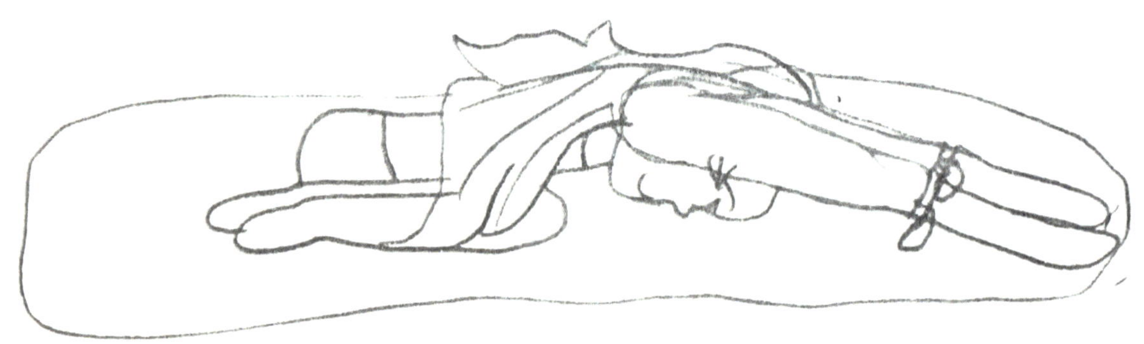

Child's Pose

I did this pose when I WAS a child. What a weird memory! Sometimes I think of the future... getting married. But... as the elders say, spend life as a child while you can! Which, well, I know!

Frog Pose

Frog pose leaps at my face like a snap of a hand!
You squat down and do the Namesta hand signal.

Warrior Pose

The warrior Princess in me drinks my tea and then
I dance to songs.
The next day I get up and go to my dance class
and I put one arm in front of me and my other
hand behind.
Then, LOL, I made the warrior pose!

Tree Pose

When I'm outside and I look up at the the trees, I lean against it and copy it. Straight, high, and cool against everything.... just like me!

Boat Pose

Boat pose probably without doubt that you'd be shaped like a boat. I love the fact that I can put my lovely cats in my lap and actually stay there!

Lotus Pose

Lotus pose makes me feel like I might explode of happiness from the beautifulness of it. The sweet, white petals are beautifully unknown destiny of stars.

Namesta

Namesta is the greeting you do in yoga. Simply say Namesta and that means all sort of greetings like, welcome, hello, or greeting. That's the main thing of yoga.

www.ingramcontent.com/pod-product-compliance
Lightning Source LLC
LaVergne TN
LVHW071231160826
845679LV00003B/958

9798363098741